PRINCESS CAN BE ON WHEELCHAIR

LIBERATION IN CONFINEMENT

SANGEETA SHARMA
'SANGAM'

To

Lord Krishna

And

My Parents

Mr. Ashok Sharma & Mrs. Yamuna Sharma

And

My Differently Abled Community.

Contents

Foreword

God has sent every living being on Earth to fulfill a specific purpose and has created everyone accordingly to fulfill that purpose only. Therefore, we have to understand that the beauty, ugliness, fairness, blackness or disability of the body does not matter because human is the best creation of God.

The best example to confirm my above statement is Miss. Sangeeta Sharma, who despite being suffering from Muscular Dystrophy since childhood, remained optimistic towards life with full faith in the justice of God.

Staying optimistic about life, she has completed her Post graduation in "Masters in Clinical Psychology" with the help of a wheelchair and want to be an IAS Officer. Due to her interest in literature, a book of poems written in Hindi – 'SARIKA' has been published in 2022. Now this, 'Princess Can Be on Wheelchair' is her second book which she has written in English. She is also a good painter.

10 poignant poems of Sangeeta Sharma are stored in 'Princess Can Be on Wheelchair.' Each poem expresses her beautiful feelings and positive outlook towards life. Her view is that we should thank God for what we have received rather than complaining about what we have not received.

There is a saying that blind is not the one who does not have eyes but blind is the one who is unable to see despite having eyes.

Sangeeta Sharma has given a poignant expression to this narrow mentality of the people in the last two poems of the collection. I pray to God to give every living being the vitality and positive feelings and optimism towards life like Sangeeta Sharma.

My best wishes to Sangeeta Sharma to achieve success in all her goals and reach the ultimate point.

Dr. Dinesh Pathak 'Shashi'

28, Sarang Vihar,

Mathura-281006

Mob-9870631805

Preface

First of all, I embrace the opportunity to express my deep sense of gratitude to everyone and my readers for sending me their appreciation and encouragement through their warm wishes for my first book **"SARIKA."** Thank you very much, it made me feel honored.

"PRINCESS CAN BE ON WHEELCHAIR" is my second book.

Might be, all of you thinking that I entitled my book, "Princess Can Be on Wheelchair."

It sounds very strange.

How can a princess be on wheelchair?

Generally we talk or read about any kingdom, we find that there is a king has a princess who is very pretty with talkative eyes and attractive hair, speaks in generous way and walks very confidently.

But we use to confine ourselves to think or write that there is a king has a princess who is very pretty with talkative eyes and attractive hair, speaks in generous way but on wheelchair.

Why can't a princess be on wheelchair?

Why it is very hard for people and society to see beauty on wheelchair?

Why it is hard to accept disability?

Disability is not a bad thing, it only need acceptance. I feel pity for society, how bad definition of beauty they percieve.

I think people are more disabling than our body.

I believe, this world will become even more beautiful when people understand the simple definition of beauty that beauty does not come solely from the body, but from the feelings of love and respect for one another, along with the freedom of expression.

For this book, I chose my painting as the cover page. In it, a wheelchair is symbolizing disability or confinement, a woman playing the violin is symbolizing self-acceptance, and music is representing the liberty that cannot be confined in any manner.

Through title, cover page, paintings of mine, poetry and expriences of my own life's journey, I tried to present, being disabled is not the matter of shame, we are more than our bodies and our existence as a human being does not solely depend on how society perceives something as beautiful and desirable.

In book, I included ten poems, first two poems titled, **"Princess Can Be on Wheelchair"** and **"Differently Abled"** are the poems which are closest to my heart because these are the reflection of mine and output of my own life's experiences.

Through these two poems, I want to tell disability is not confinement, it makes us confident and a person full of empathy.

I myself a rare girl, having Muscular Dystrophy, too has the realisations of all the hardships and emotional sufferings very well. I know how some criticisms are enough to scatter us in some situations. There are countless obstacles lying on the way such as acceptance of existence in society, limited access, lack of opportunity in education and employment due to various barriers etc.

But it is part of life, I wholeheartedly embrace this label and proud to be the voice of talented, diverse, passionate differently abled community.

Being differently abled is part of my identity and I respect my identity.

It is for my people and community also that don't focus on what you have lost just focus on what has left at your side.

If you focus everytime on what you have lost, this will create mess and enough to demolish the good side of yours.

Always believe, we are the creation of nature and nature can't be wrong.

I want the world to realize that beauty and dignity can be found everywhere- from magnificent throne to simple wheelchair.

With honor and dignity say and make the world echo,

Darling world!

Princess can be on wheelchair.

I included other poems too in this book which are throwing light on the various simple philosophies of life and are enough to make life better like,

"Born to Roar" reflects women empowerment,

"Baby Steps" emphasis on patience,

"Braille" is talking about inner light of humankind which is cover by the clouds of ignorance,

from **"It's Alright"** is echoing everything happens for a reason,

"I Want Life from Life" is reflecting value of life over materialistic world,

where **"Flute!"** is the ultimate example of willpower.

Last two poems in the book are reflecting narrow-minded perspective of people such as poem titled,

"Dear! Male Best Friend!" is about male-female friendship because friendship has no gender. It can be purely based on the understanding, empathy and compassion towards each other.
Draupadi and Lord krishna are the best example of this pure bond of empathy and compassion.

Other one is on mental health titled **"Oh! Humankind!."** Awareness about mental health is becoming our great responsibility nowadays. Our body, mind and spirit rely on mental health. We take our mental well being for granted. When it comes to physical health, we go to doctor. But when it comes to emotional and mental well-being, we don't want to seek help because fear arises that we get the label of 'mad' or 'insane' from people.
Avoid all these senseless stuff.
Your mental health must be your first priority.
It's for society also, choose your words wisely because it can have a grave impact on one's emotional and mental well-being.
Words hold immense power.
Always remember, sometimes "It's okay not to be okay."

Choose love! Choose kindness!.

It is a small step, through my book, I hope to pour some optimism into the human soul and influence stereotypical mindsets and prejudices to some extent. I hope to once again receive encouragement and blessings from my readers and everyone.

Sangeeta Sharma 'Sangam'
Email- sangeetasharmajee@gmail.com

Acknowledgements

It is my honor and I am feeling truly blessed while dedicating this book to my differently abled community, who constantly inspire me to express myself and is a great source of empathy for me.

I owe to nature that given me birth as daughter of these lovely parents (Mr. Ashok Sharma and Mrs. Yamuna Sharma). For them 'Thank you' is just a word. It is like a single drop of water into the ocean.

My mother's sacrifices and my father's faith in me are the architect of mine.

They are source of blessings and courage.

Rainbow can add seven colors only but they can add countless colors and meaning to my life.

I still don't understand from where they get the strength.

They never give up on my dreams!

Grateful for the bond I share with my sisters (Mrs. Reeta Sharma & Miss. Kavita Sharma) as well as my brother-in-law (Mr. Lalit Sharma). Each and every one is source of respect, love and care. I am blessed to be the part of this family.

Lots of love for my little Shambhavi.

Thank you so much to all my respected teachers for recognizing my talent and always inspiring me to believe in myself.

I am cordially thankful to my loved ones too who put smile on my lips, happiness in my heart and constantly making me feel confident by theirs positive energy and love.

I would like to express my sincere and whole hearted gratitude to Senior author Dr. Dinesh Pathak 'Shashi' for his kind support. I'm extremely blessed to have someone like him as my senior and guide.

Above all, it is my strongest belief, this would not have been possible without the grace of the God who always sends light on my way to make my things happen.

Just grateful towards everyone and everything!!

Thank you all, very much!!

1. Princess Can Be on Wheelchair

I am not just a body

I am a dignified soul

Don't underestimate, my existence

I am playing my beautiful role

Why you think too much,

I am rare

Darling world!

Princess can be on Wheelchair.

You see my body,

Count my flaws

I am not just a petal

I am a complete rose

I am deeply enlightened

Free like music in air

Darling world!

Princess can be on Wheelchair.

I am magnetic

Aim to attract whole world

With the wings of patience

I fly like a bird

Beautify my face,

Applying color of prayers

Darling world!

Princess can be on Wheelchair.

Liberation in Confinement.

2. Differently Abled

Ray of Life in Lifeless.

I learn, 'The Art of Living,'
Despite of having obstacles.
With smile, announcing!
Yes, I am Differently Abled.
I do my work differently,
Every day, hugging labels.
With dignity, embracing!
Yes, I am Differently Abled.

I keep Rainbow on my head,

Kissing forehead of my people.

With love, saying!

Yes, I am Differently Abled.

I respect my identity,

Voice of so many disabled.

With honor, accepting!

Yes, I am Differently Abled.

I am baugainvillea,

Thorns are inseparable.

With courage, echoing!

Yes, I am Differently Abled.

3. Born to Roar

Be Your Mate.

Being a woman

Am I born to household chores?

Shhhh

Dear society!

I am lioness, born to roar.

I am phenomenal

Hate to behave in a certain manner

Good girl versus bad girl

This game makes me bore

Shhhh

Dear society!

I am lioness, born to roar.

Tiara is of serenity

Flowers reflect bold

I love to feel the soil

Doesn't want gold anymore

Shhhh

Dear society!

I am lioness, born to roar.

4. Baby Steps

Do not hurry up,
Just dive in rest.
We can not get,
Whole at once.
Fly with baby steps.
Impossible to put whole garden,
In single, little nest
It is better to keep,
A sunflower.
Lit with baby steps.
Oceans have their own history,
They are result of
Millions of water droplets.
You, yourself is poetry
Express with baby steps.

5. Braille

She is omnipresent
But in veil,
Not the matter of seeing
She is braille.
Just feel her, in you
She is prevail
Go after her
Follow hers trail.
Once you'll get her
A fire will ablaze
She is nothing but energy
Just feel, embrace and gaze.

6. It's Alright

No need to be perfect, every time.

It's alright.

You pick wrong words.

You say 'No.'

You do mistakes.

You become selfish once, out of hundred.

Unable to make your promises fulfilled.

Prioritize yourself, first.

You say Good-bye to people,

just they're unworthy to your life.

You're getting confuse over things.

It's alright.

Because,

To get her prince,

Cinderella will have to lose her sandal.

7. I Want Life from Life

Basket of blessings,

A simple serene hive.

No mansion, no ornaments.

I want life from life.

Bouquet of emotions

May smile float in eyes!

Imprints of good deeds,

I want life from life.

May peace play in me!

Doesn't want to hectic, everytime.

Wanna a nap in moon's arms,

I want life from life.

8. Flute!

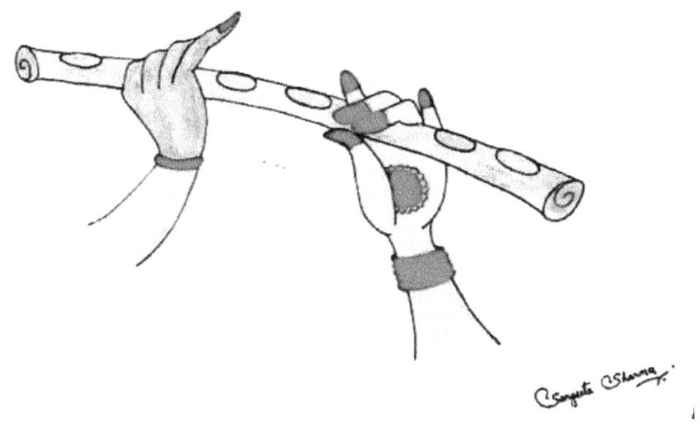

Flute: An Inspiring Parable of Willpower.

Honorable! flute!

You are inspiring parable

Every atom bears melody

You make desert, arable.

In warm, harsh conditions

You dare to write a fable

Cutting, drilling, but smiling

Gracefully, you bear unbearable.

In scriptures, on inscriptions

Soul blossoming, shying, lovable

You dissolve romance in nature

Your euphonious journey is respectable.

9. Dear! Male Best Friend!

Bond of Empathy and Compassion.

Dear! male best friend!

We near as two eyes

Rigid norms of society

Make us far as Earth-Sky.

They are unaware

A pure bond we share

When I was in dark,

A star like you there.

Unconditioned love

Myriad respect

As shield as you behave

My favourite, your embrace.

Our innocent friendship

Cover in a veil, so long

On ground of rigid norms

We can't be along.

Being a male-female

Our friendship, proved wrong

Such a stupid people

Can't see us as grown.

Friendship has no gender

It's a dedicated, beautiful boon

Forever heal your soul

Soothe like a moon.

10. Oh! Humankind!

A Human Being Is a Sheild of One's Own Self.

Oh! Humankind!

Don't be harsh, to yourself.

To heal, physical wounds

You apply ointment, very well.

But you neglect, some wounds

Engraved on mental health

Apply ointment on them, too

And heal them as well.